HARTFORD PUBLIC LIBRARY

The Orchid Family

The Orchid Family

Lynne Martin
illustrated by Lydia Rosier

William Morrow & Company   New York 1974

Text copyright © 1974 by Lynne Martin.
Illustrations copyright © 1974 by Lydia Rosier.
All rights reserved. No part of this book may be reproduced or utilized in any form or by any means, electronic or mechanical, including photocopying, recording or by any information storage and retrieval system, without permission in writing from the Publisher. Inquiries should be addressed to William Morrow and Company, Inc., 105 Madison Ave., New York, N.Y. 10016.
Printed in the United States of America.
1 2 3 4 5 78 77 76 75 74

Library of Congress Cataloging in Publication Data

Martin, Lynne.
   The orchid family.

  Bibliography: p.
  1. Orchids—Juvenile literature. I. Rosier, Lydia, illus.
II. Title.
QK495.064M37   584'.15   73-23001
ISBN 0-688-21784-2
ISBN 0-688-31784-7 (lib. bdg.)

To Jay

Contents

Orchids Everywhere 9
Orchid Plants 26
Orchid Flowers 34
Hunting Wild Orchids 51
Man-Made Orchids 67
Growing Orchids at Home 79
List of Orchids and Orchid Growers 90
Further Reading 94
Index 95

Orchids Everywhere

The orchid family is the largest of all plant families in the bright and beautiful world of flowers. In fact, nearly ten percent of all species of flowering plants are orchids. Moreover, they grow on every continent but Antarctica.

Most wild orchids, however, are found in the tropical areas of the globe, where heat is constant and rainfall plentiful. The large and showy orchids commonly seen at a florist's shop originally come from South American rain forests of Colombia, Venezuela, Peru, and Brazil. Other equally beautiful types of orchids live in the hot and humid regions of the Far East. Africa has fewer orchids than any other tropical area.

Of all the continents, Australia has the least

number of orchids. Yet the nearby island of New Guinea is immensely rich in orchid species. With some 3000 native species, this large and mountainous island has more orchid varieties than any other land. Costa Rica, a small country in Central America, is also noted for its vast and varied concentration of wild orchids. About 1200 species thrive there at all altitudes including that of the cloud forests on two-mile-high mountain slopes.

Surprisingly, the Hawaiian Islands have only three small and insignificant native orchids. The cultivation of orchids, however, is one of the Islands most important industries. Visitors are customarily welcomed in this sunny place with garlands of orchids called leis. The fresh flower necklaces are made from magnificent vanda orchids, which are raised on farms and in greenhouses. Such an orchid lei contains 200 to 300 fragrant flowers that look like purple butterflies. The flowers are so plentiful that they are sold by the pound, and quantities of them

are flown by jet to countries all over the world.

A few wild orchids are distributed worldwide, but most species live isolated from other groups of orchids. That is, certain orchids are found only in Asiatic lands and others only in the Americas. Some orchid habitats are even restricted to one island in the Pacific Ocean or a particular mountain peak in Peru. There is an orchid that only grows on the branches of calabash trees in tropical America.

A plant's habitat is its home, or natural environment. Since orchids are found growing from sea level up to 14,000 feet, the range of their habitats is wide. The climate changes with altitude on a mountainside, and the orchids that grow wild at ground level differ from orchids in the Alpine habitat on top of a mountain.

Relatively few orchids — around 160 species — grow in Europe. In the United States, every state has at least an orchid or two. Ninety different kinds are native to Florida. The showy

lady's slipper—*Cypripedium reginae*—is Minnesota's state flower.

In tropical rain forests, most orchids dwell high up in the treetops, where there are generous amounts of sunshine, cool breezes, and sheltering foliage. And though they seem delicate and fragile, some hardy orchids inhabit the frigid valleys of Alaska and Greenland, as well as the snow-covered peaks of the Himalayas.

Orchids grow in parched deserts and in moist swamps, bogs, meadows, and woods. Two extremely rare Australian species spend their entire lives underground. Not a particle of these subterranean plants is green; at most, only the tiny flower heads reach the surface of the soil.

The best-known and most popular orchid is probably the cattleya (*cat*-lee-uh), which grows in tropical America from Mexico to Peru. Pale purple in color, the flower has a ruffled trumpetlike petal flanked by gracefully arching petals and is big enough to cradle in two hands. Some people call it the queen of the orchids.

Yet orchid flowers appear in every color. In size, the plants range from midgets less than an inch tall, with flowers smaller than a ladybug, to monster vinelike orchids that spider their way over forest tree branches for a hundred feet or more. Certain orchid blossoms measure almost a foot across.

Whatever their appearance, all orchids are members of a single plant family, the Orchida-

cattleya

ceae (or-kid-*a*-see-ee). Some of their relatives are banana plants, lilies, palms, and bamboos. All belong to the class of flowering plants called "monocots," which are distinguished by having only a single seed leaf. A seed leaf is an embryo plant surrounded by stored food, like a kernel of corn. From it come the first leaves.

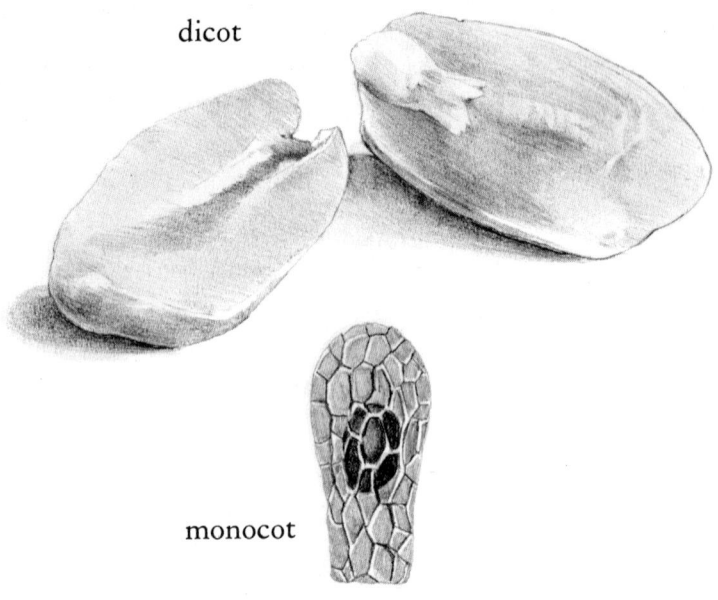

The other class of flowering plants is called "dicots," and they have two seed leaves in the embryo. The two halves of a peanut, a bean, or a walnut are the seed leaves of typical dicots. Plants in each group differ in the structure of their stems, leaves, and flowers too.

Orchids are commonly divided into only two groups, despite all their apparent differences.

Those that grow in the ground are called "terrestrials." They are earth dwellers, which sink their roots into the soil and shoot up like ordinary plants. Most of these plants are equipped with underground stems called "tubers." Some look like onions, and they store food for the plant. Such orchids are usually native to colder regions and temperate climates. Lady's slippers belong to this division of orchids.

Asiatic lady's slipper

Those that grow in elevated positions on trees and rock cliffs are called "epiphytes." Their name comes from the Greek. *Epi* means *outside* or *on*, and *phyte* means *plant*. Cattleyas belong to this division of orchids.

Epiphytic orchids are not parasites. They do not take food from the tree on which they grow, but merely use it as a platform with exposure to the sun. A single tree in the tropics may support fifty different orchid species as if they were colorful birds roosting among the leaves. Trees often become so burdened with orchids and other epiphytes that branches collapse under their weight.

These orchids are also sometimes found growing outside the forest. They spring from a thatched roof of a hut in Java or bloom along a fence in Bali. They have been seen on telephone wires in Panama. One orchid hunter tells of discovering an orchid growing on a skull found in the wilds of Burma.

The *method* of growth determines whether an orchid is a terrestrial or an epiphyte. Each of these groups is further divided into two types, according to the structure of the plant.

Orchids such as vandas or lady's slippers have a central stem that grows straight up and lengthens season after season. They are called "monopodials." Monopodial means *one foot,* and the classification includes those plants with a single base like a tree. Leaves and blossoms sprout along the main stem. Most monopodials produce flowers in sprays or clusters toward the top half of the plant.

Plants with a creeping stem that grows in a lateral fashion are called "sympodials." This main stem puts out new growth on a seasonal basis, then branches into a special swollen stem, which grows upright. Each new erect stem grows its own leaves and flowers. Cattleya orchids are an example of sympodial growth.

There are then four basic types of orchid plants: sympodial epiphytes, monopodial epiphytes, sympodial terrestrials, and monopodial terrestrials. Altogether they total over 660 genera (plural of genus) and about 25,000 species. Their classification is based on where and how they grow and what they look like.

The two units of an orchid's scientific name

monopodial   sympodial

indicate the genus (a group that shares characteristic features) and species (a group that shares the same individual features) to which it belongs. The name is Latin or Greek, and it remains the same the world over in all languages.

For example, one orchid is named *Oncidium crispum.* The first word, *Oncidium* gives its genus, which is unusually large and includes 750 species. The second word, *crispum,* gives the species and emphasizes a particular quality of this flower's petals.

Sometimes the scientific name comes from the name of a person or place connected with

the flower's discovery. Then it is given a Latin ending to make it conform with botanical language. Cattleyas, for example, are named after William Cattley, a famous British horticulturalist, who first discovered and raised these flowers in 1824.

Orchids often have nicknames in addition. One flower is commonly known as the dancing lady orchid because of its resemblance to a miniature ballet dancer. The common names of other orchids likewise stem from their distinctive patterns, shapes, or features. There are spotted leopard orchids, dove, scorpion, spider, butterfly, swan, and rattlesnake orchids. A certain flower is known as the veiled nun, another as flying duck, and still others as shadow witch, rattail, and Punch-and-Judy orchids.

Diuris maculata, the common donkey orchid from Australia, has two earlike petals. The orchid named *Dendrobium cucumerinum,* the cucumber orchid from Australia, has leaves with the tiny bumps and shape of a pickle.

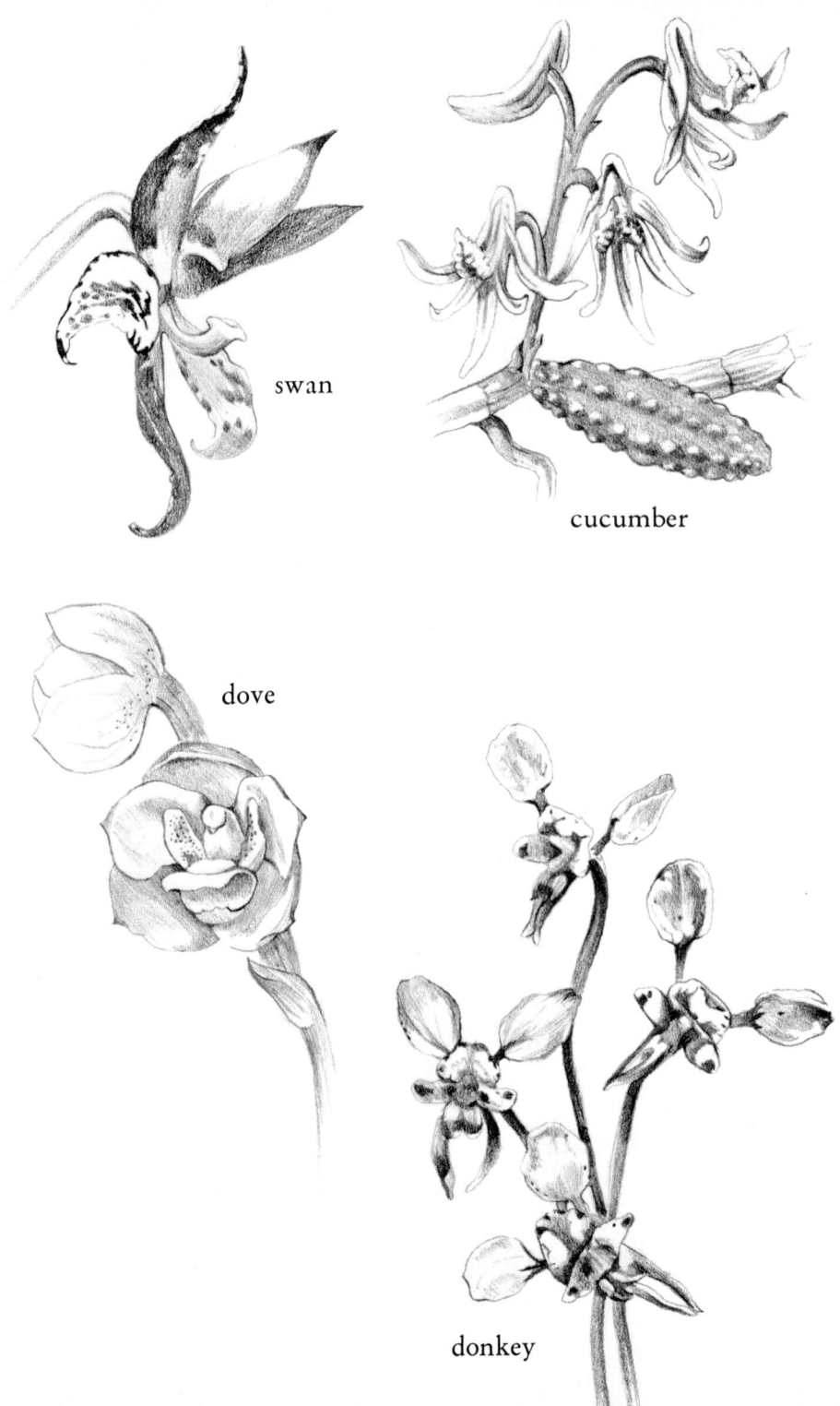

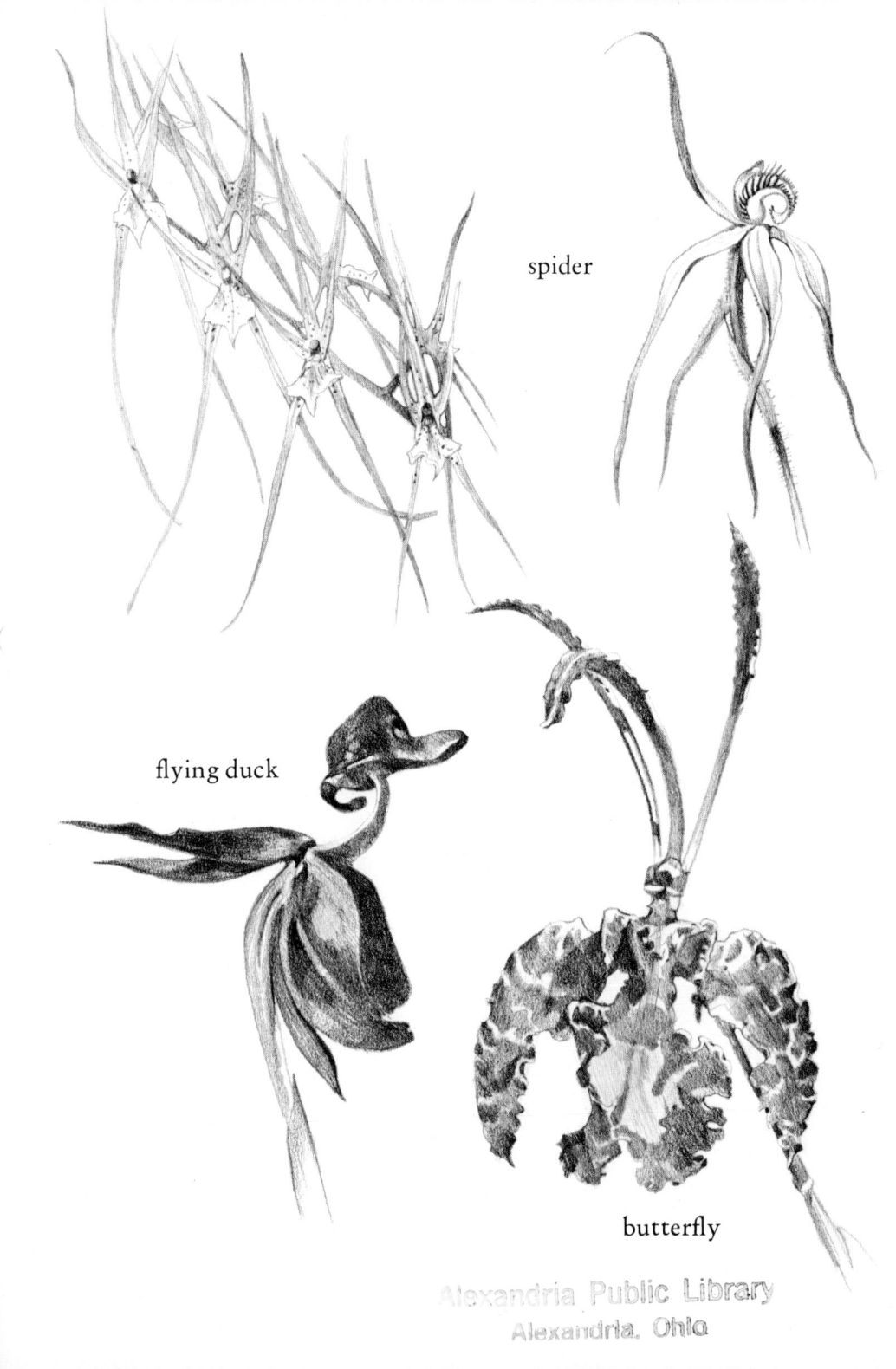

Orchid Plants

In the warm regions of the earth, where they are the most numerous, orchids mainly grow as epiphytes, or air plants. They seem to float in the air on their perch in the sky. How did they get there? And how do they survive?

When an orchid seedpod is ripe and splits open, seeds by the thousands ride the wind. In one species of Venezuelan orchid, a single seed capsule contains some four million seeds. These vast numbers of seeds produced by orchids are needed for their survival.

The germination of orchid seeds is uncertain for a number of reasons. Orchid seed is the smallest of all seeds in the flowering world; they are as fine as grains of face powder. The drift of pale gold released by the seedpod is

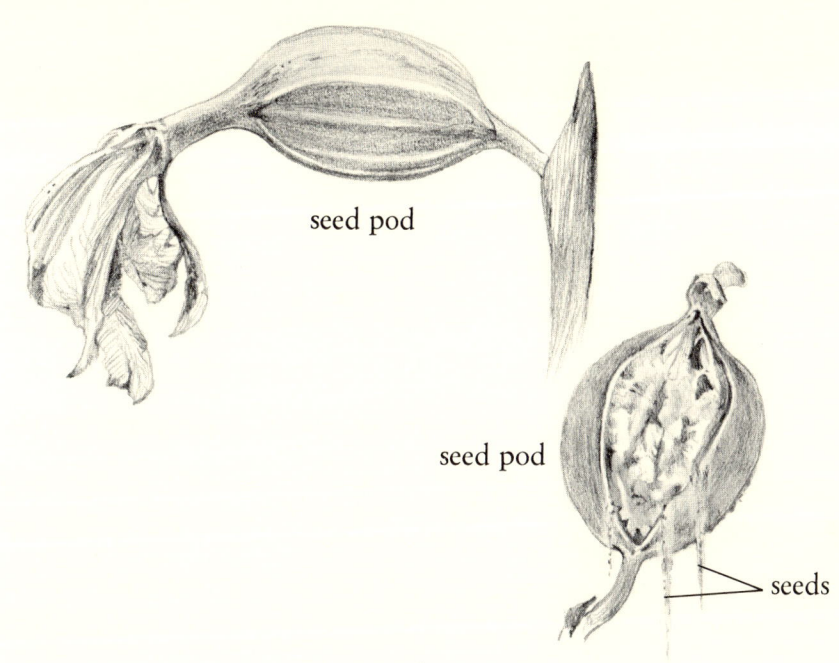

seed pod

seed pod

seeds

picked up by moving air currents and dusted from high branch to branch in the forest. If seeds are blown far from the forest or land on the ground, their prospect for growth is dim. Not enough sun filters through the trees whose crowns huddle together hundreds of feet in the air and form a dense green roof in the forest.

Unlike most seeds, the weightless orchid seeds contain almost no nutrient for the embryo plant. They do not have enough stored food to continue to develop by themselves once they start to grow. The seeds must settle on fungus-laden bark or rock. Only the hyphae, or fungal threads of certain species of fungi, will boost orchid seeds into life. The microscopic fungus invades the seeds and stimulates germination by supplying special minerals and moisture until the seedling is established enough to make its own food. Thus, the moldlike partner temporarily carries out the function of roots.

Orchid plants need the same mineral foods, light, and water that all plants need. Instead of sending their roots down into the soil to pick up the minerals, they send out a network of roots over the bark of the tree or rock on which they grow. When it rains, dust that has blown up onto the tree is washed down to these roots. Rotting bark and fallen leaves, dead insects, bits of flowers, bird droppings and other decaying matter also accumulate on bark or rocks and nourish epiphytic orchids. From drops of water and spoonfuls of forest debris, a small but suf-

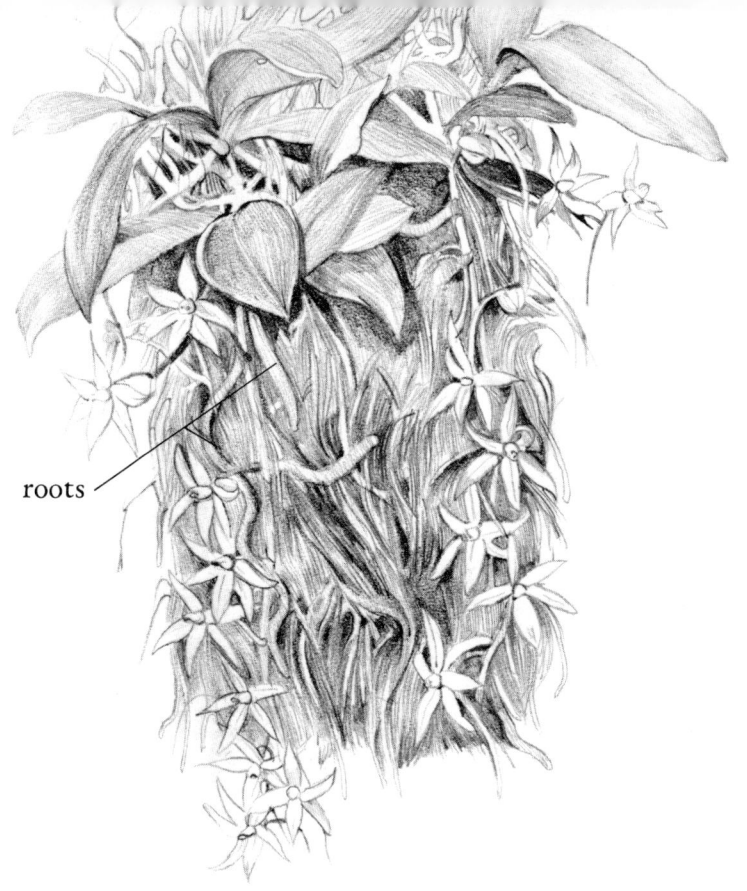

roots

ficient environment, riddled with fungus growth, builds up.

An orchid plant does not reach full-flowering splendor for a long time. The cattleya orchid, for example, takes five to seven years. Even when it is a year old, the seedling is only one-half inch tall. But as time passes, a sturdy plant forms. The orchid develops thick stems, leaves, and more roots, which hang out in the air and soak up moisture from frequent rains, dew, and the always-humid atmosphere of the rain forest. These are aerial roots; other roots anchor the plant to its perch and absorb necessary nutrients.

These aerial roots are brittle and white with the thickness of a lollipop stick. They manufacture food materials and absorb water from the damp air through a spongy covering called the "velamen," which acts like an ink blotter. When saturated, they turn pale green.

The main root-bearing stem of a cattleya is called a "rhizome," and it rests on the bark surface. Periodically, during the plant's growth, the rhizome sprouts swollen upright stems at intervals along its length. In time, these stems will bear leaves and flowers.

These chunky stems are called "pseudobulbs" (*soo*-doh-bulbs), which mean *false bulbs.* They are so named because they are true stem structures in function and not bulbs at all. Pseudobulbs

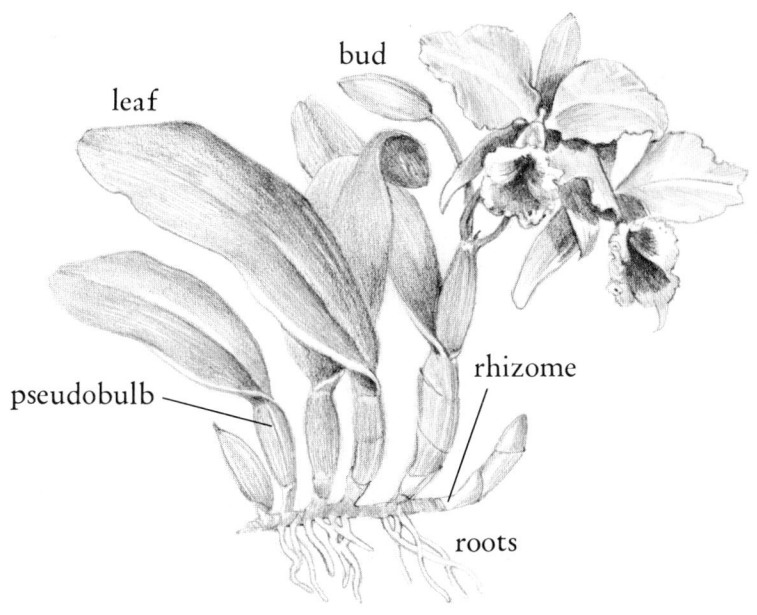

vary in shape and size among the orchid species. Some are the size of a child's head, some fifteen feet long, others the size of a pinhead. Cattleya pseudobulbs vary from four inches to three feet, depending on the species.

Orchids have developed reservoirs in the form of these thickened stems and their fleshy leaves, which store both food and water and keep the plants from drying out between rains. In the rain forest orchids are drenched by rain every day. But perched high up in the airiest places, epiphytes live in a drier atmosphere than ground vegetation, which is never dry at any time of the year. The plants are somewhat like cacti, which have to store what water they get for use over a long period.

Most orchids are evergreen plants, but some species are deciduous and drop their leaves. These orchids depend on their pseudobulbs to survive periods of drought.

When a leaf pokes through the top of the pseudobulb, it is thick, spatula-shaped, and a bright, shiny green. The waxy texture makes orchid leaves resistant to drying and discourages insects from eating them. Like other monocot leaves, the veins run parallel along the length of the leaf from base to tip.

Seven years pass. Bloom stalks now arise from the top of the pseudobulbs, bearing one to thirty buds, depending on the species. Each bud gradually, over a six-week period, fills a paper-thin sheath, which protects it.

The colors are pale when the flower begins to open, but grow more intense as the hours pass. In twenty-four hours the flowers are fully expanded. They will stay in bloom for a month or more. Plants in the orchid family may produce a solitary exquisite bloom or fragrant clusters, while others have short or long arching sprays of flowers.

As orchids are perennials, they continue to thrive year after year.

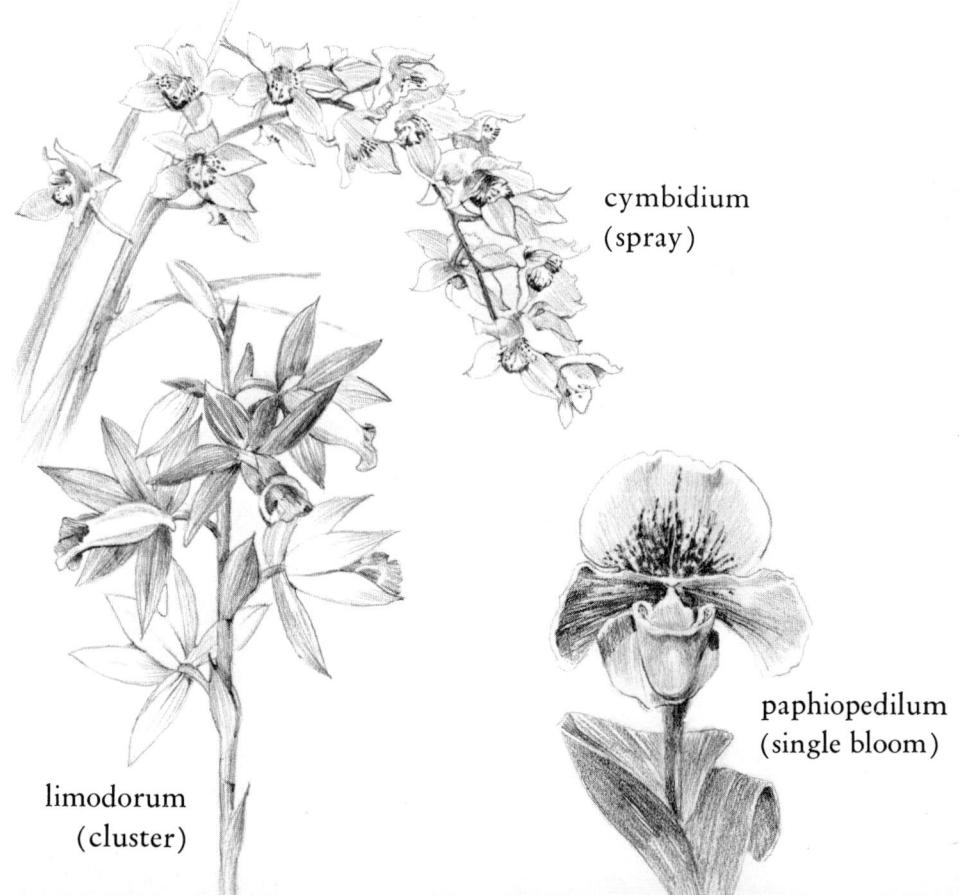

cymbidium
(spray)

paphiopedilum
(single bloom)

limodorum
(cluster)

Orchid Flowers

Like any flower, an orchid is a modified stem that has developed specialized leaves at the tip, the petals. Every orchid flower has three sepals and three petals, even though these flower parts may be joined, reduced, or enlarged in size, and they vary in form.

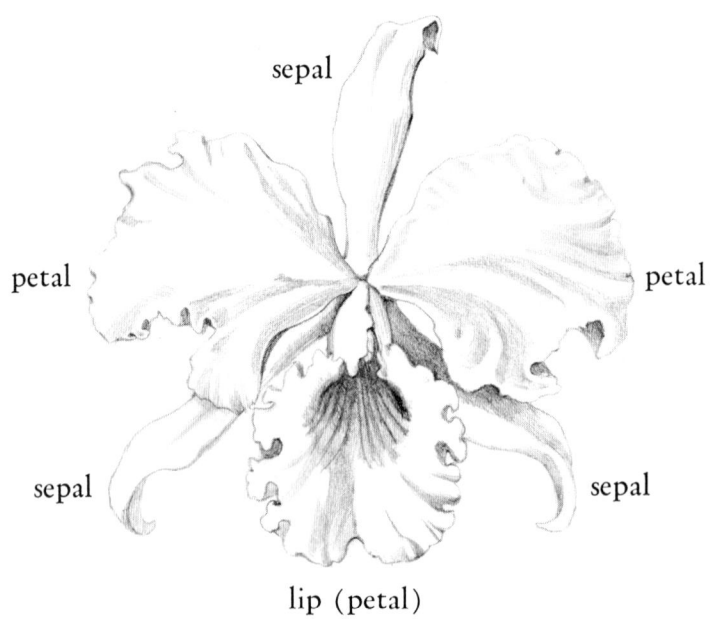

The sepals, which are almost always colored, protect the flower in the bud stage and support the inner ring of three petals. The two side petals are usually identical, while the third, lower petal always differs in shape. This often larger and more showy petal is called the "lip," or "labellum." It may be modified into a trumpet-shaped tube, as in the cattleya, or it may resemble a pouch or slipper, as in the lady's slippers. It can also assume various other shapes, with fringes, tassels, or streamers, and be decorated with an interesting color pattern.

The petals play an important part in the reproduction of the plant by attracting insects to the flower with bright colors and pleasant fragrances. They serve as a landing platform for the visitor in search of nectar. The contrasting markings of spots, lines, and squiggles guide the insects to the reproductive organs in the heart of the flower, much as the twinkling landing lights at an airport show the pilot where to come down.

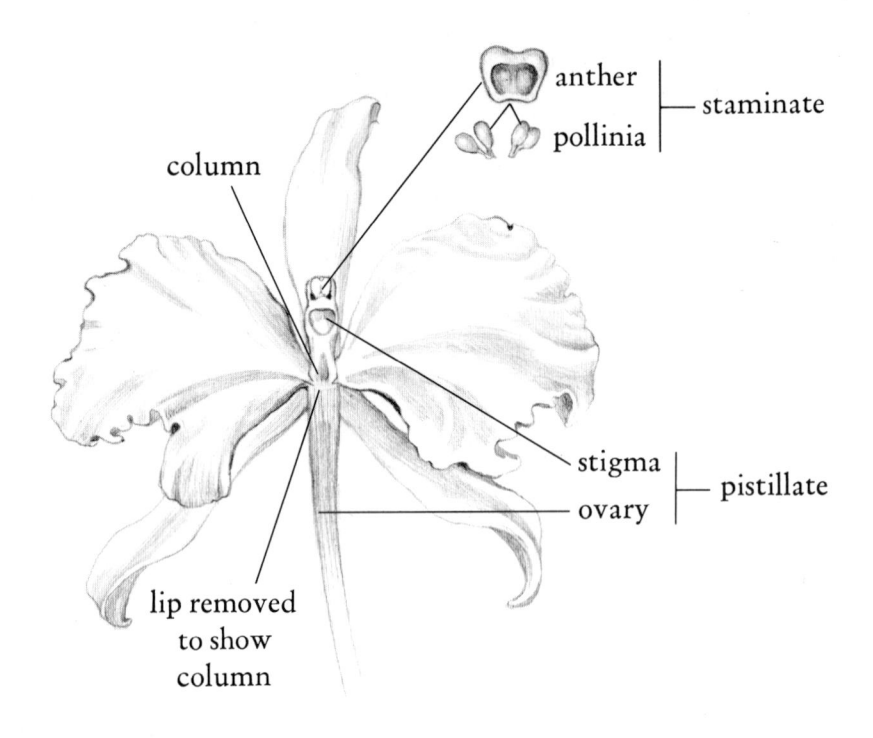

Diagram labels: column; anther; pollinia; staminate; stigma; ovary; pistillate; lip removed to show column

Orchids are unique in that the male (staminate) and female (pistillate) organs fuse to form a single prominent sexual column. The staminate parts include the pollen and the knobbed end of the stamen called the "anther." The pistillate parts include the stigma and the ovary. The orchid's fleshy column, shaped like a club, is usually located either within the tube of the lip or directly above the lip of the flower. At the tip of the column is the anther. Here pollen grains are clumped together in two to eight waxy pellets called "pollinia," which are covered by a tiny hinged pollen cap.

A partition called the "rostellum" separates the pollen-bearing male portion of the column from the female portion below it. The rostellum oozes a fast-setting gluelike substance that affixes the pollen masses to insects seeking nectar. The stigma is a deep dent on the surface of the column filled with sticky liquid. When the same insect enters another flower, the pollen is transferred to the stigma, and the flower is pollinated.

Farther down the column lies the ovary, where ovules, or egg cells, are found in tremendous numbers. Only when the male cells contained in pollinia unite with female cells in the ovary is the orchid fertilized and able to produce life-bearing seeds.

Seeds are ripened ovules; seedpods, the fruit of the plant, are ripened ovaries that contain the seeds. Some pods expand to the size of a lemon, and those of most types of orchids take from nine to twelve months to mature. The pod turns brown, and cracks appear in the grooves along the sides. When the pod bursts apart, seeds by the thousands are dispersed in the wild green world.

Among the flowering plants, pollination is the sexual process that assures reproduction of their kind. In the case of the orchids only about three percent of the species self-pollinate. In these instances, the flowers have developed devices allowing the pollinia-bearing column to curve downward to brush against the stigma. But most orchids are constructed so that they cannot be fertilized by their own pollen. Instead, the pollen masses are fastened to a visiting insect as it backs out of the flower. When the insect enters another flower, the golden pollinia is forced into its stigmatic cavity.

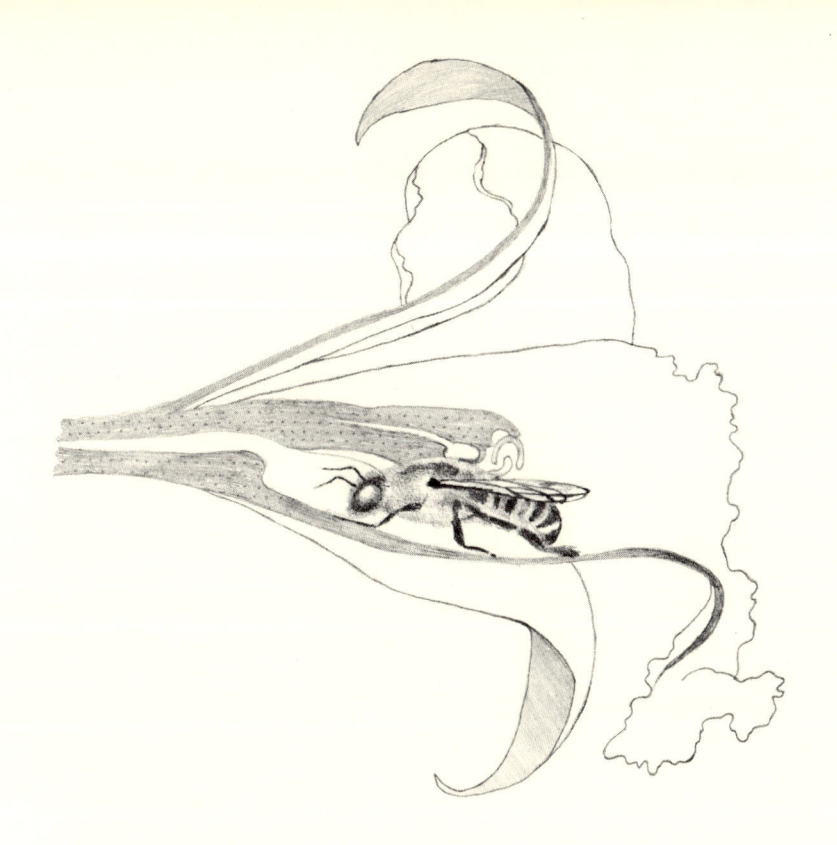

This kind of pollination is known as cross-pollination, and it is the basis of plant evolution. It enables plants to improve their heredity and to produce new forms to meet the changes in their environment. The variety of colors, shapes, and sizes among the orchids result from their cross-pollination and help them to survive. All these adaptations in the flowers are ones that appeal to the pollinating birds and insects.

The most common orchid pollinators are bees, wasps, butterflies, moths, flies, mosquitoes, and birds; bees predominate. Most orchids are adapted to a specific pollinator, which only visits flowers in the same species. Bees usually stop at flowers of only one species during a particular flight. Even though a second orchid species is similar in color and grows close to a first orchid species, the bees regularly skip it. Other bees will pollinate the second species.

There are remarkable examples among the orchids to illustrate how perfectly the flowers and pollinators are made for each other. Each orchid's pollinating mechanism will work only if an insect of just the right shape and size enters the flower. A tiny orchid, just one-quarter inch in diameter, needs a very small insect. If the kind that can serve as bearer of its pollen does not come along, the flower may wither and die, even though it is visited by many insects.

More than a hundred years ago, when the famous scientist Charles Darwin studied the

Charles Darwin

pollination of orchids, he visited the island of Madagascar along the coast of Africa. A beautiful orchid called *Angraecum sesquipedale* grows there. The seven-inch flower looks like a six-pointed star and is of such heavy texture that it seems to be made of white wax. A long slender spur, or nectar tube, extends from the flower.

What type of insect, Darwin wondered, could possibly pollinate this flower? What insect could reach the nectar in the bottom of the

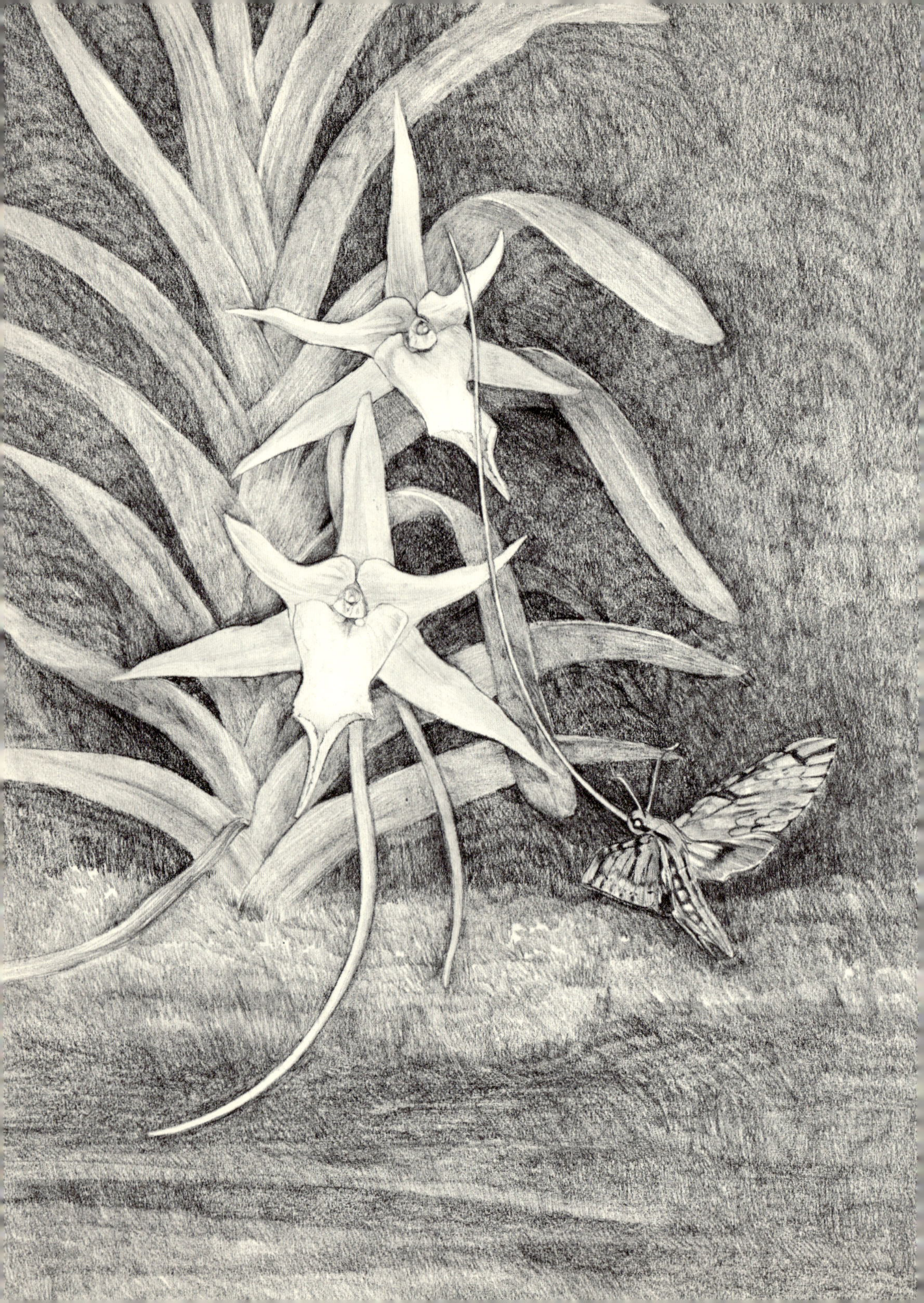

eleven-inch spur? The opening of the spur was too small for most insects to gain entrance.

After some deliberation, he reached a conclusion: only a large moth with a proboscis (tubelike sucking mouth) the length of the spur could pollinate the flower. But no such moth was then known to science. Forty years later, however, Darwin was proved right. A moth exactly fulfilling his description was discovered on the large island by another scientist. The giant moth had a six-inch wingspread and a proboscis eleven inches long.

Many other orchids also require a special kind of insect to pollinate them. The brown bee orchid (Ophrys) is a small, metallic-colored flower that grows in Europe. Furry brown male bees busily zoom into flower after flower. What beckons the bees is the shape and scent of what seem to be the females of their species. The flowers are such an exact replica, even to petals that look like the hairy antennae of bees, that male bees attempt to mate with the flowers.

Other orchids appeal to the food-hunting instincts of pollinators. The lip of the bearded orchid is studded with bristles. The glossy hairs of the beardie, as Australians have named the flower, imitate a caterpillar, prey of a wasp. Thus, the wasp is attracted to the flower. Another orchid displays tiny spots that look like spiders on its petals. A spider-hunting wasp dives at the dots and departs with pollen glued to its body. When the wasp visits the next orchid looking for spiders, a pollen exchange is made.

bearded

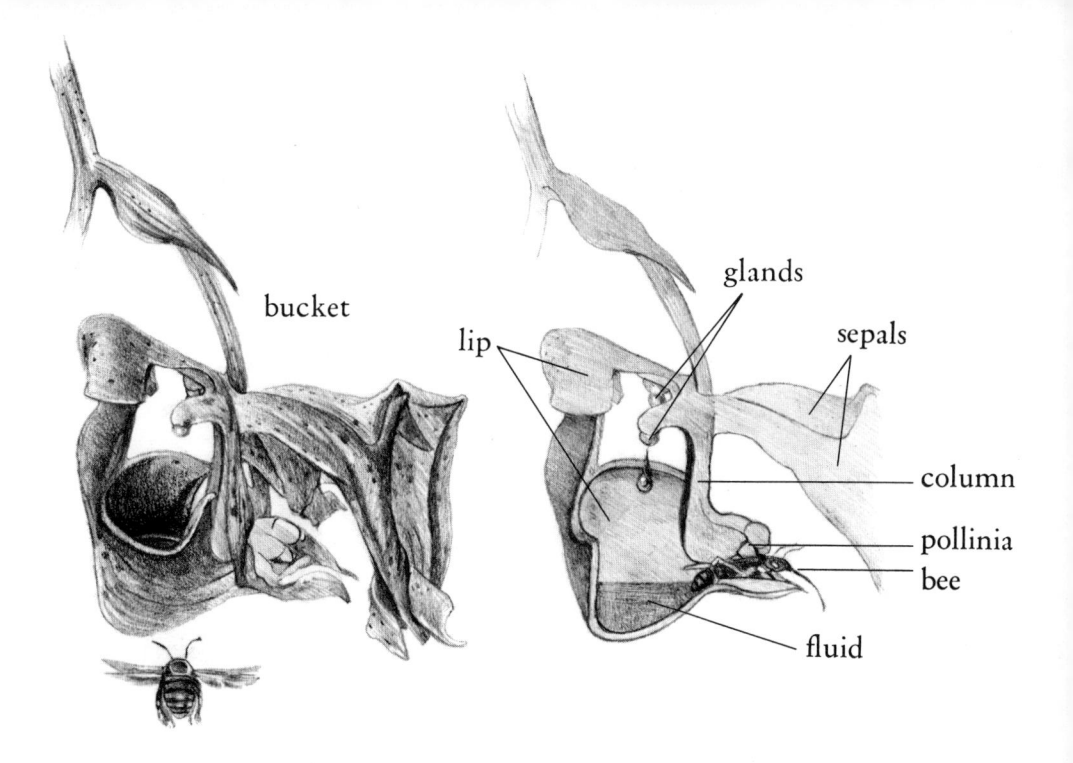

The story of the bucket orchid's pollination is even more incredible. A bee lands on the bucketlike lip of the flower. It skids down the waxy surface into a pool of fluid secreted by the flower's faucet glands. To escape drowning, the insect exits by way of the spout of the bucket. As it crawls out, the insect brushes against pollinia and bears the pellets away.

Both the flying duck and an orchid known as the greenhood have a sensitive lip that acts as a

lip open   lip closed

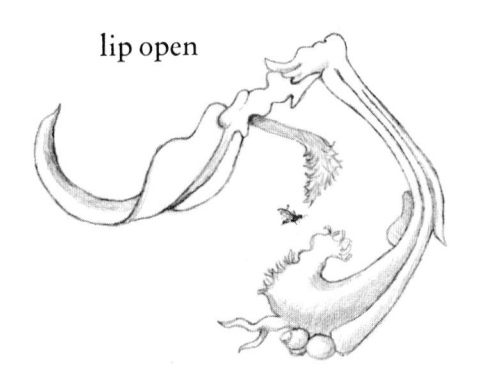

trapdoor when insects as light as gnats or mosquitoes land on it. The hinged lip springs shut, flipping the insect into the flower. The only way out is through a tunnel ingeniously stocked with pollinia.

Color, either vivid or pale, is what attracts some pollinators. White orchids are more visible in darkness and are pollinated by night-flying moths. Pale lady-of-the-night orchids reinforce their attraction to moths by sending out a perfume after the sun goes down.

Scarlet orchids whose blossoms droop in a nodding position grow in Brazil. They attract hummingbirds, which whir beneath the flowers and probe into them for nectar. *Beija flor,* or flower kissers, is what Brazilians call these birds. Not only does the drooping position of the red orchid cater to the hummingbird's habit of hovering and approaching flowers from below, but the color is right. Red is the brightest part of the spectrum to birds; hence these orchids are bright and conspicuous to the hummingbird.

cinnabar gnome

Other orchids in Mexico directly appeal to bumblebees. These particular flowers are curved to suit the shape of the bee. Furthermore, the flowers are purple, thus catching the attention of the bumblebee whose eyes are sensitive to violet and ultraviolet colors.

All colors of the rainbow in all shades from bright to pastel are represented in the orchid family. Every variation exists except for black. There is a myth about black orchids, but there is no such flower. Some orchids, however, are such a dark maroon or purple or mahogany that they appear to be black.

Shades of green and brown, rather than the familiar pale purple, predominate among orchids in the wild. True pink and blue are perhaps the rarest colors. Many orchid flowers are a combination of colors, made even more ornamental by contrasting dots, splotches, veins, and other markings.

Fragrance — not color, shape, or size — is the primary attraction for many insects, since it is

cinnamon-scented

associated with their nectar-food. Sometimes the flower's scent is delicate, sometimes very strong. Some orchids smell like cinnamon.

Not all orchids are a delight to smell, though. In the genus *Bulbophyllum,* there are species known as frog orchids. They are small and unattractive with unpleasant odors. One African frog orchid is said to smell "like dirty feet."

Another orchid from Borneo, according to one scientist, bears an odor that reminds him of the putrid smell of a herd of dead elephants. But flies, which are attracted to the foul odors of decaying matter, are compelled by the smell to enter the flowers and thereby pollinate these orchids.

As Darwin noted long ago, "Orchids in the plant kingdom are as varied as any of the most beautiful adaptations in the animal kingdom. . . ."

Hunting Wild Orchids

For centuries, like sleeping beauties, epiphytic orchids remained a hidden treasure in the wilderness. Their discovery was not to come until repeated explorations unveiled the natural riches of all the tropical continents.

Orchid appreciation of the terrestrial types goes back to the time of Confucius around 500 B.C. According to the writings of this famous Chinese sage, the acquaintance of good men was like entering a room full of *lan,* or fragrant orchids. Long a favorite of Chinese and Japanese artists, orchids have been the subject of many of the finest Oriental paintings.

The ancient Greeks, however, were the first to take botanical notice of these curious plants. Writing of European ground orchids, Theophrastus, known as the Father of Botany, gave the name *Orchis* to the plant.

Superstitions about the medicinal powers of various parts of the orchid plant were widely believed in then. The Greeks and, later, medieval people thought that if a pregnant woman ate the young, firm underground tubers of an orchid, she would give birth to a male child. If she ate the older, softer round bulbs, she would bear a daughter.

Men in Malaya chewed orchid roots, then sprinkled the "powerful" particles over a sick elephant to cure it. The Indians of North America boiled the roots of the lady's slipper with maple sugar as a headache remedy.

The tribe of cave dwellers called the Tasadays, who as recently as 1972 were discovered living in the wilderness of a Philippine Island rain forest, use orchids in different ways. Naked except for orchid-leaf loin covers, the men gathered before a fire to steam tadpoles wrapped in orchid leaves for an evening meal.

We even eat orchids. In some lands, succulent orchid leaves are cooked as vegetables. The rhizomes of certain orchids are dried and ground into a bland cereal. The flavoring in vanilla ice cream, at least the best kinds with little brown flecks, comes from the cured seedpod of an orchid.

Some 450 years ago, Spain's conquistadors found the Aztecs of Mexico adding bits of an orchid's fragrant seedpod to their cocoa. Their source was vanilla orchids, which also flourished on the island of Madagascar. Raising orchids to provide vanilla extract became a thriving industry in both lands and still is so today.

The vanilla flower lasts only a day and must be pollinated by hand on large plantations or in greenhouses. The flowers do not all bloom at the same time. So every day workers go from flower to flower, lifting the little tongue on the flower column with a pointed stick and pressing

vanilla

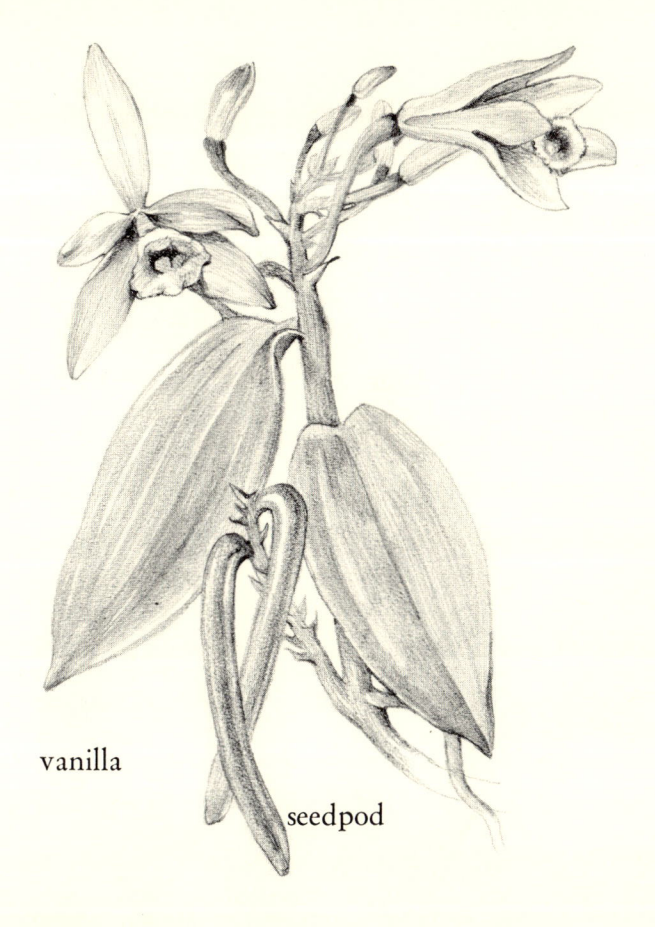

seedpod

the pollen-bearing anther and stigma together. They call it "marrying the orchid," and a good matchmaker can pollinate 2500 flowers in one day. In the wild probably no more than half a dozen flowers on a plant would be pollinated by tiny bees.

The green seedpods, shaped like a slim banana seven inches long, are gathered before they are fully ripe. Each one is packed with innumerable tiny black seeds, with hard outer seed coats, unlike typical dustlike orchid seed. At this time the pods have no flavor or aroma.

When ripe, the pods are spread out to cure

under the hot sun for six months. To guard against theft, growers prick their initials in the pods for identification. The pods shrivel somewhat and turn dark brown. The vanilla beans, as the seedpods are sometimes called, are then ready for the extraction of the flavoring.

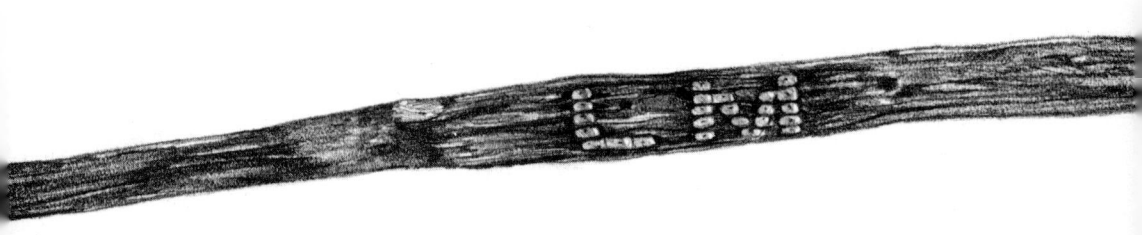

Only a few of the sixty-five species of vanilla orchids have any economic value as the source of vanilla extract. At present, they are the only orchids that yield a commercial product other than their flowers.

The first appearance of tropical orchids in Europe came about by accident. In the late eighteenth century some shriveled specimens were used to wrap other plants taken from a

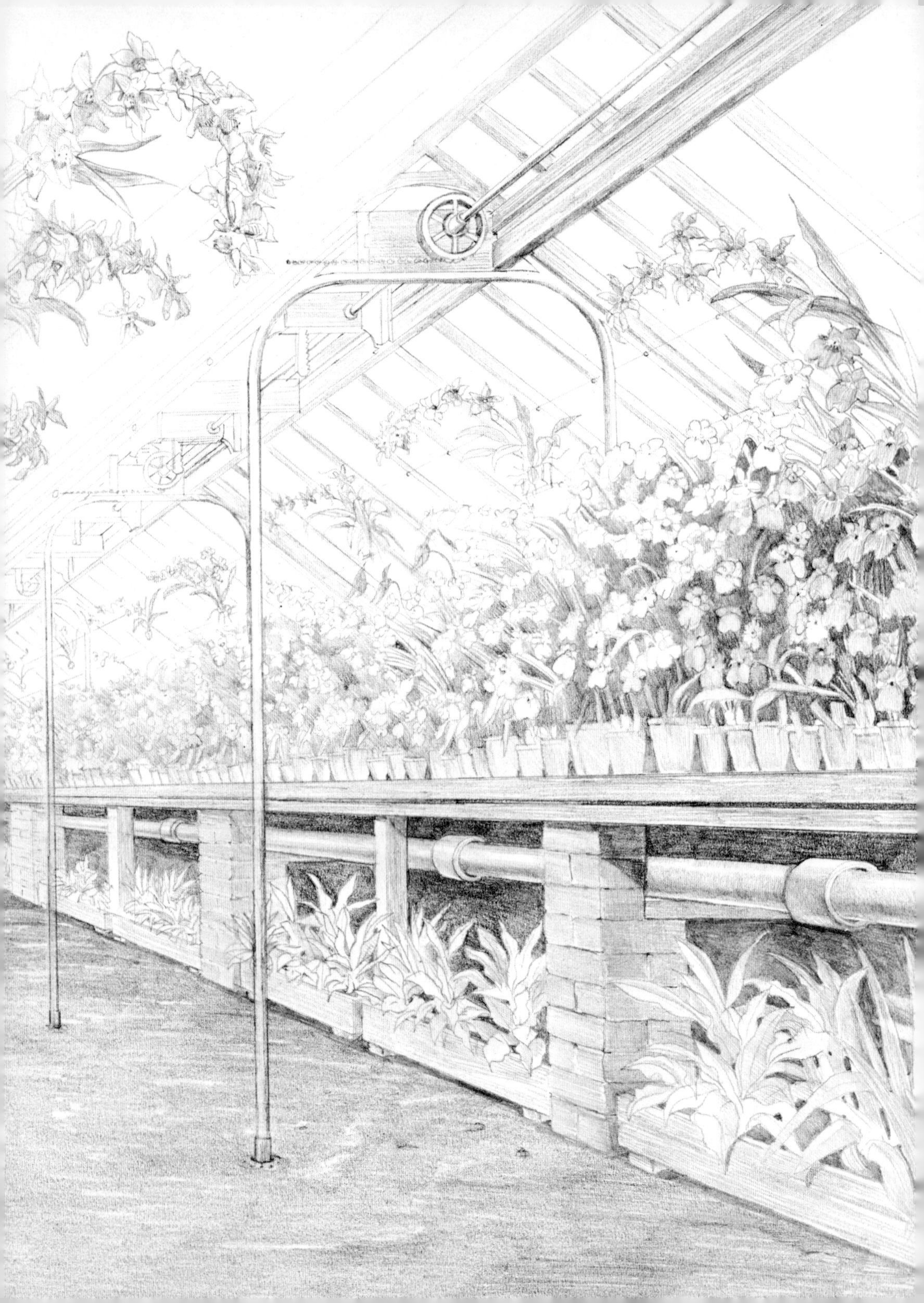

tropical rain forest and brought to England. There a horticulturalist carefully nurtured the plants until they finally bloomed.

People with a passion for beauty were overwhelmed by this new plant. Some early greenhouse men did not know how to cope with orchids, however. They mistakenly kept their "stoves," as they termed their hothouses, tightly sealed, damp, and as warm as possible. Most of the orchids died with this treatment. "I had caught my orchid," one of these early growers remarked, "but how to treat it I knew not."

Then one pioneer lowered the greenhouse temperature and admitted air, thus duplicating the natural treetop conditions of wild orchids. Through trial and error the growers discovered the many specialized techniques essential to raising these unique plants, using the proper light, water, air temperature, and fertilizers to produce flowers.

Gardening indoors became a fad during Victorian times in the late nineteenth century.

Nurserymen encouraged European aristocrats to raise exotic plants. As rare tropical varieties became status symbols, collectors competing for botanical prizes undertook long and hazardous expeditions searching for orchids in the rain forests around the world.

In those days a rare orchid plant in prime condition might bring a price of $500 to $2500 at the going rate of exchange in London. These plants were sold at auction to commercial growers and wealthy amateur horticulturalists. One species, *Odontoglossum crispum,* brought an orchid grower a small fortune. In 1904, the plant was sold for $5000, the equivalent of $25,000 today, one of the highest prices ever paid. Orchids were a symbol of luxury, and the rich wanted to collect them as people today collect fine paintings or rare jewels.

Before long orchid hunting became a wholesale business. More orchid hunters were dispatched to the tropics. The men returned with plants by the tens of thousands. When one ex-

Odontoglossum crispum

plorer finally tracked down an orchid called *Cattleya rex* in Peru, he gathered the incredible number of 17,000 plants of this species.

In these early days the orchid hunters faced a plant-choked, insect-ridden, snake-infested wilderness without a clue to where the orchids were. Often they became lost or fell ill with fever; many died, victims of tropical diseases.

Sometimes in parties or in pairs, hunters hacked paths through the dense undergrowth armed only with a machete. Month after month they slept in hammocks and lived in huts made of bamboo trunks lashed together with vines from the forest. They rode muleback. Sweat ran down their ears, which were bleeding from insect bites and scratches. They paddled up remote tributaries of the mighty Amazon River in South America, endangered by bloodthirsty piranha fish, beset by treacherous river rapids and whirlpools. During the rainy season the river rose thirty feet and thousands of miles of forest were flooded, forcing fierce ants and many snakes into the trees with the epiphytic plants.

Orchid hunting was an exhausting quest. Even when the search was successful, there was still the task of getting masses of plants down from the lofty trees or scaling steep, rock-faced cliffs to reach them.

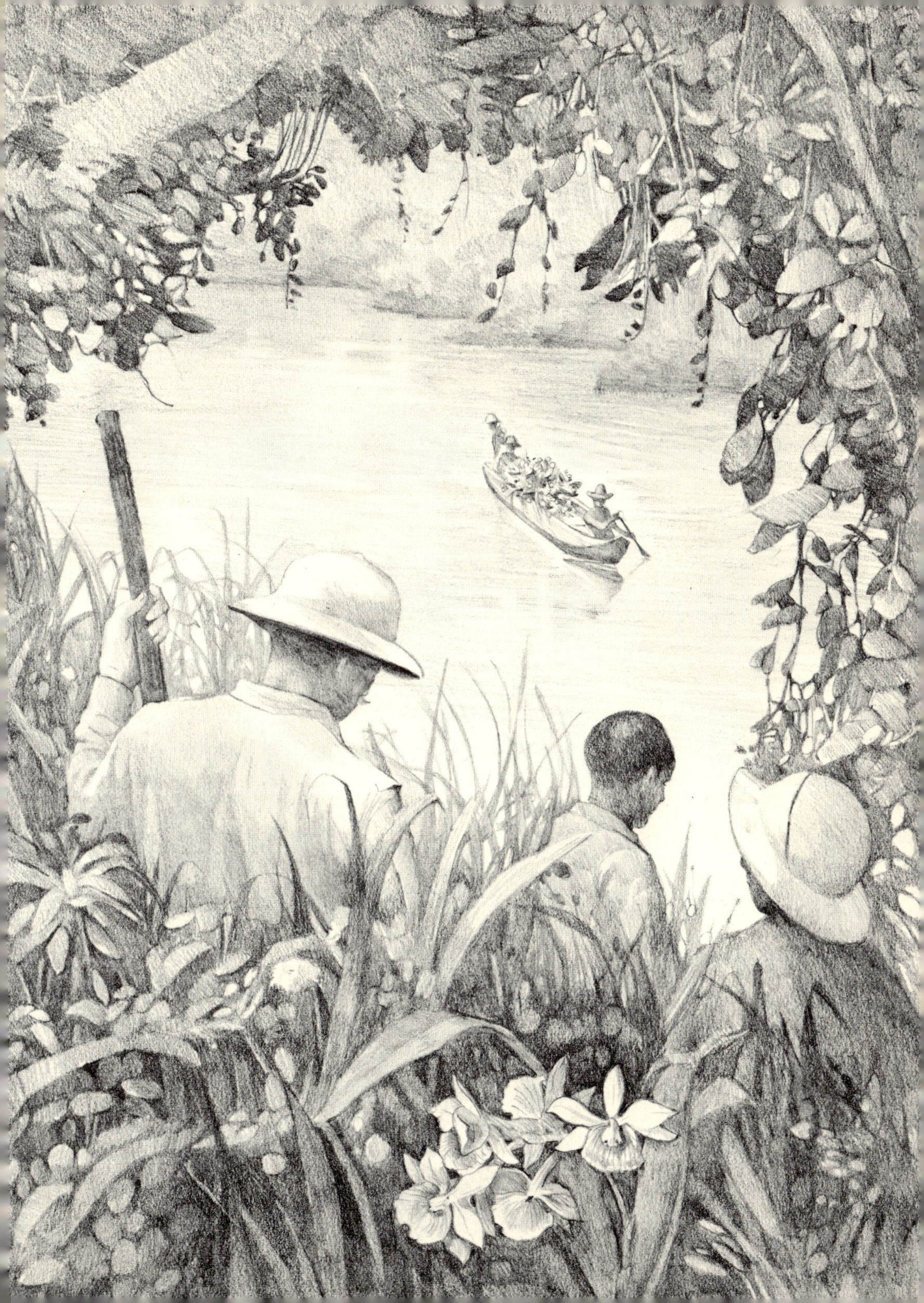

At camps established in the forest, the plants were washed and trimmed and packed in wood shavings, forty to a slatted wooden case. Each twenty-by-twenty-by-thirty-inch case weighed eighty pounds when packed, making an ideal cargo for a mule. The difficult journey continued as the valuable collections were hauled out of the wilderness for shipment by river boat to a large port, followed by a long ocean voyage.

Interest in these exotic plants, indeed almost a mania, lasted into the early twentieth century, by which time many Americans were also hunting for wild orchids.

Today, however, the days of massive collecting for commercial use are over. In countries where orchids grow, extensive export of orchid plants is prohibited. Special permits are required to collect specimen plants. Expeditions still go forth, but modern orchid hunters are usually scientists from universities, museums, or botanical gardens.

One scientist recently searched for orchids in

Venezuela and found the biggest single orchid plant he had ever seen. It was encircling a tree trunk sixty feet above the ground. In an operation that took nearly an hour, a man in the group climbed the tree, detached the plant with a machete, and lowered it to the ground in a rope sling. This specimen, *Cattleya gaskelliana*, was four feet across, took four men to carry it, and bore 150 purple blossoms. When the plant was separated into three portions for packing and transport, the men quickly discovered hundreds of *Melipona* bees swarming in the root mass. Luckily these bees don't sting.

Man-Made Orchids

Why was the hunt for orchids so popular? Why were so many plants taken, and why such high prices obtained for them? Men simply could not raise orchids the way they cultivated other flowers. The only available plants were hidden far away in the forest.

Growing orchids from seed was almost impossible in the early days of orchid culture. Gradually many dedicated men began to unravel the secrets of successfully propagating orchids in a greenhouse environment. German and French scientists found out that a certain fungus sometimes helped orchid seeds to germinate, and they worked out a very involved method of growing orchids in flasks inoculated with this special fungus.

Then, in the 1920's, Doctor Lewis Knudson at Cornell University demonstrated that the fungus was not absolutely necessary for orchid seed to germinate. He proved that the primary cause of the difficulty was due to the inability of the orchid embryo to manufacture its own food. The function of the fungus was to convert complex starches into simple sugars for the seed to use as food.

So this American scientist mixed a formula of nutrients with agar, a product of seaweed, added plain sugar, and sowed orchid seeds on it.

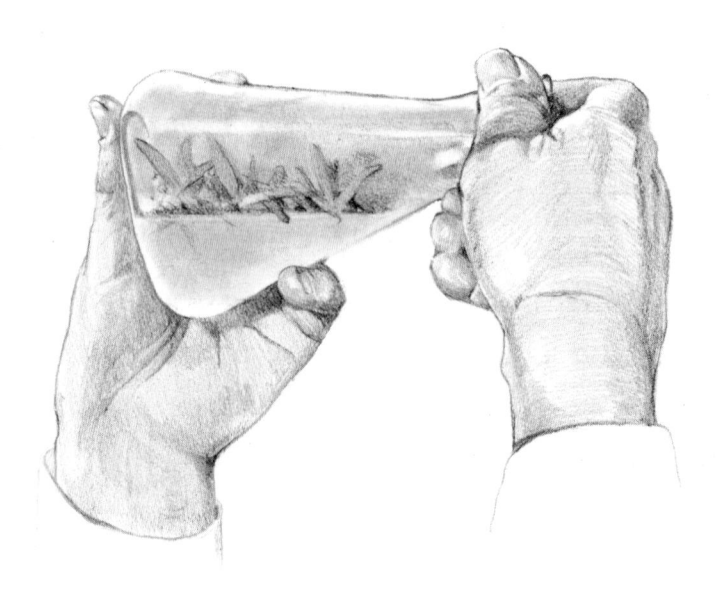

(Nowadays orchid growers add green coconut milk, tomato juice, or bananas to boost the germinating seed.) The seeds were isolated in sterile glass vessels and kept in a moist place with subdued light for several months to a year. When roots and leaves formed, they were ready to be transplanted into three-inch community pots with about twenty-five other plantlets. As they grew they were graduated to plant pots of their own.

Though orchids can be propagated by dividing the plant, quantity production is accomplished by growing them from seed. The process is slow and tedious. Cattleyas take from five to seven years to reach the flowering stage as they do in the wild. The phalaenopsis orchid requires two to three years, and other orchids need varying lengths of time to mature.

Unlike other flowering plants, orchids could not be crossbred (hybridized) at first. That is, gardeners could not pollinate a flower from one species with pollen from another species or even

hybrid
(*sophrolaeliocattleya*)

another genus. By producing what is called a hybrid, growers try to create an improved species. They could not do so in the case of the orchid, however, since they did not know which were the male and female parts.

At last an English surgeon with botanical training successfully analyzed the strange sexual column of the orchid, which included both stamen and pistil. Then gardeners were able to crossbreed two different species of orchids. Quickly they began to select desirable traits and crossbreed orchids as other men bred horses or dogs.

Since orchids are both male and female in the same flower, gardeners use either of two plants for either sex. In any particular crossing the plant that carries the seedpod is called the female. The plant that supplies the pollen is called the male. Growers pollinate a flower within the first week that it is open, within the first three days if possible.

First, they remove pollen from the female flower before they insert pollen from the male flower, so the two do not mix. Then they cut off the sepals and petals, including the lip of the flower, to make correct placement of the pollen easier.

The pollen from a valuable plant can be refrigerated and stored for later use. It can be shipped around the world, so that breeders can take advantage of stud plants with fine qualities developed many thousands of miles away.

Once pollen is transferred to the stigma, male sperm cells in the pollen move downward inside the ovary to fertilize the egg cells there.

The ovary enlarges steadily as it matures over a period of from nine to twelve months into a seedpod.

Growers can check seed under a microscope to see if it has life. Bad seed without embryos is usually white. Live seed has a fat and swollen embryo in the middle of its long and narrow length and is darker in color, usually tinged with red, yellow, or brown.

Through hybridization by orchid growers we now have many new and finer orchids of every size, color, and shape imaginable. Orchid breeders throughout the world register their hybrid successes with an internationally recognized firm in England. They list the parentage of the cross, the date it was made, the date of the first flowering, and a description of the first flowers.

In this way they get credit for their creations and save others from repeating what has already been tried. Sometimes the flowers are named after them.

Before 1900, 200 hybrids were registered. Today more than 35,000 crosses are recognized. No other plant family has produced as many hybrids. There are more man-made orchids than natural species in the wild, and the number grows each year. Some native species of orchids are grown commercially, but most of those sold today are hybrids raised in greenhouses or outdoors in warm climates.

Today another growing technique called "meristem (from the Greek word for *divisible*) culture" is also practised. By means of this reproduction process countless young orchids identical to a single parental plant can be produced. Tissue that is the basis of new growth within the shoots of plants is cut out, placed in bottles with nutrient solutions, and then rotated on a wheel to expose it constantly to fresh nutrients. The growth cells reproduce themselves continuously. At a certain point, cell clusters are formed. These clusters are removed and left to rest with another nutrient. The separated bits of cells develop into plantlets that will produce flowers exactly like those on the original plant.

Growers provide florists with all orchid varieties today, but the most popular are the showy cattleya orchids, or "catts," whose ancestors came from the tropical American rain forests. Supplying cut flowers is a multimillion-dollar business.

In flower shops an orchid corsage costs ten dollars or more. Phalaenopsis, the moth orchid, as well as others are used in bridal bouquets. Cut flowers for home floral arrangements often include orchids such as cymbidium, paphiopedilum, odontoglossum, oncidium, and cypripedium.

epiphytic

In parts of California and in Florida people grow epiphytic orchids in coconut shells or baskets fastened to trees in the garden. They also cultivate terrestrial orchids among other plants on the ground. Orchids such as vandas, laelias, phalaenopsis, dendrobiums, cattleyas, epidendrums, and many other genera thrive in warm and humid climates all year round. One vanda orchid has been growing on a tree in Florida for more than twenty-five years and often blooms with 150 or more flowers at a time. The plants are sturdy enough to endure occasional cold spells and even violent hurricanes.

In practically every part of our country there are orchid growers who conduct a large business shipping orchid plants of various species and sizes to orchid hobbyists. Many thousands of amateur orchid growers belong to the American Orchid Society, located at Harvard University in Cambridge, Massachusetts, or local orchid societies in their communities. Some have such fine specimens that they win prizes at regional or national flower shows. There are indoor gardeners who are content with a few potted orchid plants and others who spend thousands of dollars for large collections of orchids that they house in elaborate climate-controlled greenhouses.

Kew Gardens, the Royal Botanic Gardens near London in England, is famous for its collection of orchids from every region on earth, though it specializes in Asian and African orchid species. Orchids of the Americas are emphasized in the collection at the Botanical Museum at Harvard University.

There may be a botanical garden, an arboretum, or a commercial orchid grower near you. There you can enter a world like the rain forest, warm and humid, full of splendor, and see for yourself the elegance of these strange and interesting flowers.

Growing Orchids at Home

Anyone can raise orchids. If you are enough of an indoor gardener to grow philodendron, you can raise exotic rain-forest orchids in the same environment that is comfortable and healthy for you.

Regular home temperatures of 60 to 80 degrees Fahrenheit are fine for most orchids. At night they should be cooler just as you like to sleep in a cooler room. Orchids are rather tolerant and even tough, so they can adjust to many conditions. Of course, they are most rewarding and will flourish best in the home given the proper amounts of sunlight and air, water and humidity.

Orchid growers all over the United States can supply plants for as little as fifty cents to as much as hundreds of dollars. Higher prices are paid by commercial breeders and large collectors for plants that they will use to breed and to show. Seedlings cost a small amount, but they are years away from flowering. Mature orchid plants are usually available from five to thirty dollars apiece. These include varieties of cattleya, laelia, and other large orchids suitable for corsages. Dendrobium, phalaenopsis, oncidium, and vanda orchids that bloom in sprays and clusters are also available. By far the most popular and usually considered easiest to grow of all orchids are the cattleyas.

vanda   dendrobium

Carefully packed orchid plants can be shipped anywhere with guaranteed safe delivery. They can be shipped in bud to bloom soon after arrival. Plants come in the pot. All you have to do is unpack them, set them in a sunny window, and follow the simple growing instructions. Growers can supply catalogs of their plants, supplies, and prices, and they are generally helpful with advice and information.

These are general rules that apply to most orchids:

Light: Most orchids, particularly cattleyas, want considerable sunlight, if possible four to five hours a day. Sunlight is very important for proper plant growth and good flowering. Since orchids grow most actively during the morning hours, set the plants next to a screened east or south window. They should be far enough away from the window glass so that they do not get intense heat from the sun, or brown scorch spots will develop on leaves. The leaves turn yellow when a plant has too much light.

With too little sun, the plant is tall and spindly, the pseudobulbs are slender, the leaves long, narrow and soft, and deep green in color. A plant grown in ample light is shorter, with thick, stocky pseudobulbs and broad, tough leaves that are shiny grass green in color.

Ventilation: Remember that orchids are basically air plants. They need air to keep them supplied with carbon dioxide essential to growth. A stagnant, stuffy room is not good for orchids. A room with good air circulation should be satisfactory, although some people set fans near their orchids. Stagnant, moist air allows the growth of fungi molds. Air should get under and around the pots. Plants can be set on an upside-down plant pot or hung in the air in a wire holder. Orchid pots may be placed on hardware cloth (strong, wide screening) over a dish of water or on a dish of pebbles. They should never be allowed to stand in a puddle of water. Avoid drafts and sudden changes in temperature.

Humidity: No expensive equipment is necessary or advisable to provide humidity for your orchid plants. The lack of humidity or moisture in the air in the average heated home is the main problem when growing house plants of any sort. But the solution is simple and easy. Take a large cake pan, Pyrex baking dish, or fiber-glass tray that is shallow and wide enough to hold your plants. Fill the pan with tiny stones, gravel, shells, or brightly colored aquarium stones. Next fill the pan about half full of water, replenishing the water as it evaporates. Place the pan in a sunny window, and arrange your pots on top of the gravel. Be sure the pots sit above the level of the water. They

should never be in the water. This is the safest and best way to supply humidity and good ventilation for orchids growing in your home. Some people also spray the foliage.

Water: Probably the most important and different thing about orchid culture is that their special type of roots must dry out thoroughly between waterings. If they are kept constantly wet for very long, the roots will rot. Orchids resist dryness better than wetness. Never use icy water on plants; water should be at room temperature. Water generously—two to three quarts per pot—but then do not water again until bone dry. Pots dry more rapidly in warm, bright weather than in cool, cloudy weather. Plants will probably need more water in summer than winter. Large pots dry more slowly than small ones. Different potting materials dry out faster than others. If the pot feels clammy and cool, then it is still damp inside. If it feels dusty-dry and as warm as room temperature,

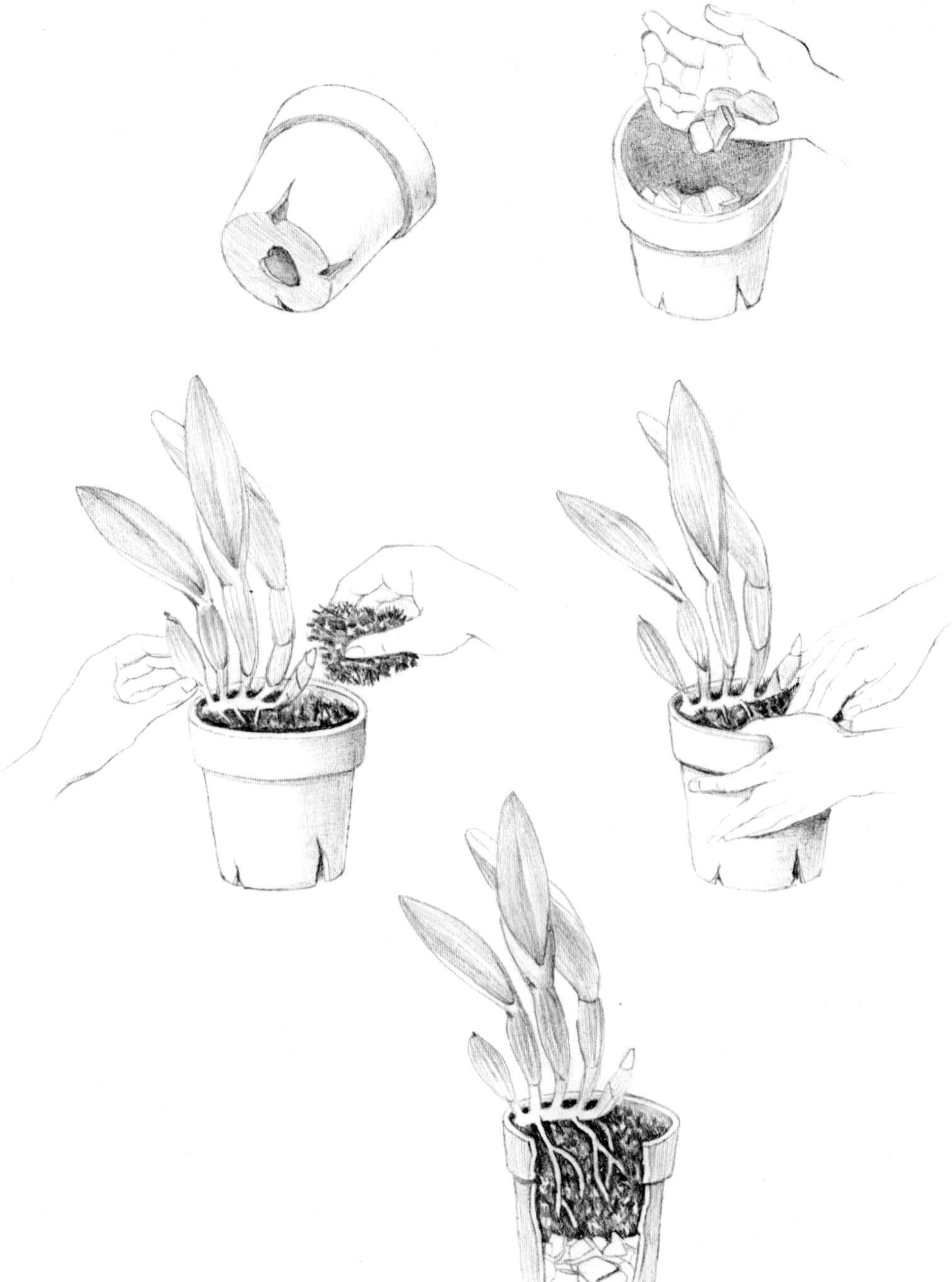

then it is ready to water. The best time to drench plants is in the morning, and you can do so in the sink or laundry tub.

Potting: Ordinary flowerpots may be used with the drainage hole enlarged at the bottom to provide better aeration for the plant. Orchid pots usually have extra slits in the base. Clean, broken clay-pot pieces should fill one third of the bottom of the pot for drainage.

Orchids are grown in a variety of porous potting materials. All of them provide the drainage and aeration necessary, yet retain sufficient moisture for the plants. Osmunda fiber (a coarse black fiber, the roots of a fern), shredded fir and redwood bark, and a new inorganic man-made lava material are all in common use. Some growers mix in perlite or peat humus. These materials are packed snugly around the roots of the plant so that the roots and the rhizome, which rests on the surface, cannot wiggle or move in the potting material. Since the rhizome, which bears the roots, is a stem structure, it must not be completely buried. It rests in a groove on the surface to prevent rotting.

Food: Orchids are usually supplied with minerals in the form of fertilizers that can be dissolved in water. These nitrogen fertilizers or fish emulsions are diluted or mixed with water and used every other time the plants are watered. Some plant foods are used monthly and are available wherever plants are sold.

Orchids are strange plants with interesting foliage and exquisite blooms. They are not as delicate as most people think and will do better if neglected than if fussed over. Living with a part of a tropical rain forest in your room is fun. If you enjoy growing plants, why not raise orchids?

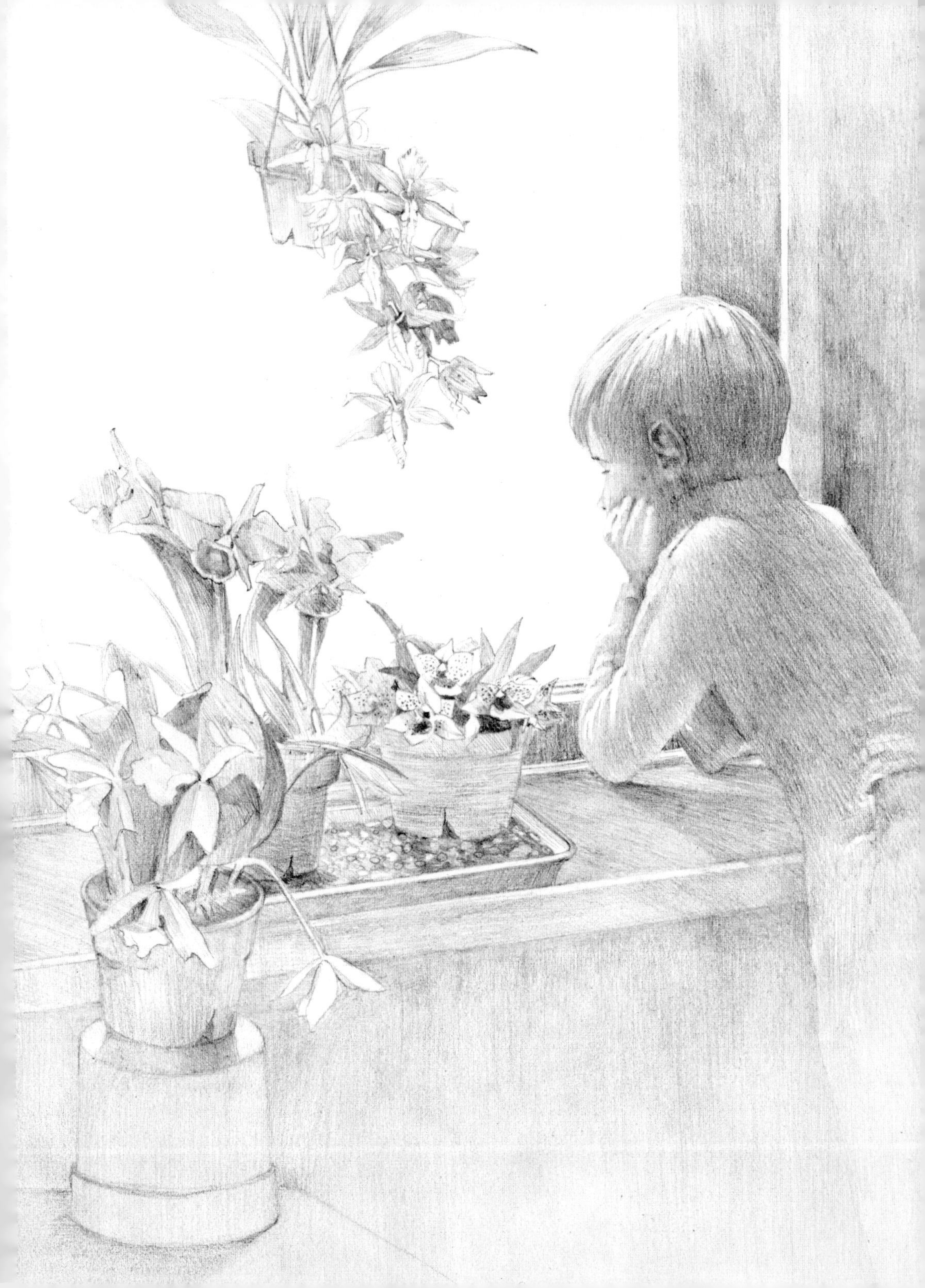

List of Orchids and Orchid Growers

Some Well-Known Orchids and Their Range

Genus	*Range*
Angraecum 200 species	Africa, islands of the Indian Ocean
Brassia 50 species	Tropical North, Central, South America
Bulbophyllum 1000 species	The Americas, India, Africa, Australia, S. East Asia
Cattleya 65 species	Tropical North, Central, South America
Cymbidium 70 species	Africa, Australia, China, Japan, India

Cypripedium 50 species	India, China, Japan, North America, Europe
Dendrobium 1500 species	Asian tropics, Australia
Epidendrum 1000 species	Tropical Americas
Habeneria 500 species	Worldwide range
Laelia 75 species	Tropical Americas
Masdevallia 300 species	Tropical Americas
Maxillaria 300 species	Tropical Americas
Odontoglossum 300 species	Tropical Americas
Oncidium 750 species	Florida, West Indies, Mexico, Central and South America

Paphiopedilum 50 species	Australia, tropical Asia, Pacific Islands
Phalaenopsis 40 species	Australia, islands of Pacific Ocean
Vanda 70 species	Tropical Asia
Vanilla 65 species	Africa, tropical Americas

Orchid Growers

Local orchid growers or florists may supply plants, or they can be ordered from the following growers:

Fennell Orchid Co., Inc.
The Orchid Jungle
26715 S.W. 157 Avenue
Homestead, Florida 33030

Arthur Freed Orchids, Inc.
PO Box 635
5731 South Bonsall Drive
Malibu, California 90265

Kiesewetter Orchid Gardens
223 I.U. Willets Road
Albertson, New York 11507

Shaffer's Tropical Gardens, Inc.
1220 41 Avenue
Capitola, California 95010

Fred A. Steward Orchids, Inc.
PO Box 307
1212 E. Las Tunas Drive
San Gabriel, California 91778

Thomas Young Orchids, Inc.
Union and Harris Avenues
Middlesex, New Jersey 08846

Further Reading

Fennell, T. A. *Orchids for Home and Garden.* Rinehart & Co., N.Y., 1959.

Northen, R. T. *Home Orchid Growing.* Van Nostrand, Princeton, N.J., 1962.

Shuttleworth, Zim, Dillon. *Orchids.* Golden Press, N.Y., 1970 (paperback).

Index

indicates illustration

Amazon River, 62, 63*
American Orchid Society, 77
anther, 36*, 37, 55
bud, 31*
Cattley, William, 23
color, 14, 33, 39, 46, 48
column, 36*, 45*
common names, 23
Confucius, 51
cross-pollination, 38-39
culture, *see* propagation
Darwin, Charles, 40-43, 41*, 50
dicot, 16*
epiphytes, 18*-19, 20, 26, 28, 32, 51, 62, 76*
flower, 32-35, 33*, 34*
flower sheath, 31*
fragrance, 46, 48-50, 49*
germination, 26-28, 27*
gland, 45*
greenhouse, 58*, 73
habitat, 9-10, 12-14, 17, 26

Harvard University Botanical Museum, 77
history, 51-54, 52*, 57-66*, 61*, 63*, 65*
home growing, 79-89, 83*, 84*, 86*
hunting, 60-66*, 63*, 65*
hybrid, 70*, 73
hybridization, 69-73
Knudson, Lewis, 68
leaf, 31*, 32, 82
lei, 10
lip, 34*, 45*-46*
medicinal powers, 52-53
meristem culture, 74
monocot, 15, 16*, 32
monopodials, 19-20, 21*
naming, 22-23
orchids, kinds of
  bearded, 44*; brown bee (Ophrys), 43; bucket, 45*; butterfly, 25*; cattleya, 14, 15*, 18*, 20, 23,

95

29*-31, 35, 69, 74, 76, 80, 81; *Cattleya gaskelliana*, 65*-66*; *Cattleya rex*, 61; Christmas star (*Angraecum sesquipedale*), 41, 42*; cinnabar gnome, 47*; cinnamon-scented, 49*; cucumber, 24*; cymbidium, 33*, 75; cypripedium, 75; dendrobium, 76, 80*; donkey (*Diuris maculata*), 24*; dove, 24*; epidendrum, 76; flying duck, 25*; lady's slipper, 13*, 17*, 19-20, 35, 53; laelia, 76; limodorum, 33*; *Odontoglossum crispum*, 60, 61*, 75; *Oncidium crispum*, 22*, 75, 80; paphiopedilum, 33*, 75; moth (phalaenopsis), 69, 75, 76, 80; spider, 25*; swan, 24*; vanda, 10-12, 11*, 19-20, 76; 80*; vanilla, 54-57*, 55*, 56*

Orchidaceae, 14
ovary, 36*, 37, 71-72
perennial, 33
petal, 23, 34*-35
pistillate, 36*

pollen, 36, 37, 71
pollination, *see* reproduction
pollinia, 36*, 45*
pollinators, 40-48, 42*, 45*, 47*, 50*
propagation, 57-78, 68*, 70*, 72*
pseudobulb, 30-31*, 32, 82
reproduction, 35-50*, 36*, 39*, 42*, 44*, 45*, 46*, 47*
rhizome, 30, 31*, 87-88
roots, 28-30, 29*, 31*
Royal Botanic Gardens, 77
seedpod, 26-27*, 38, 55*, 56-57, 71
seed, 26-28, 27*, 37-38, 56, 72
sepal, 34*-35, 45*
shape, 39
size, 14, 39
staminate, 36*
status symbol, 60
stem, 19-20, 30, 34
stigma, 36*, 37, 38, 55, 71
sympodials, 20, 21*
Tasaday tribe, 53*-54
terrestrials, 17, 19, 20, 51, 76
Theophrastus, 51-52
tubers, 17